# INTERRUPT THE SKY

# INTERRUPT THE SKY

John Hazard

STEPHEN F. AUSTIN STATE UNIVERSITY PRESS

For more information:
Stephen F. Austin State University Press
P.O. Box 13007 SFA Station
Nacogdoches, Texas 75962
sfapress@sfasu.edu


Managing Editor: Kimberly Verhines
Cover Design: Sandra Carranza
Distributed by Texas A&M Consortium
www.tamupress.com


ISBN: 1-978-1-62288-949-5

# Acknowledgments

Some of these poems have appeared or are forthcoming in the following literary magazines, sometimes in slightly different forms.

*Ascent:* "Hemlock, Finch, October"

*Arts & Letters:* "Hills," "Night Sky, Atlantic Coast"

*Atticus Review:* "Dog Thoughts," "Gulls," "Sparrow Shadow, Florida," "The Generous Marsh of Me"

*California Quarterly:* "Schenectady"

*Concho River Review:* "Volunteer Fire Department"

*Diagram:* "Flight"

*Front Range Review:* "A Flock of Starlings Forms," "Three Eggs, Florida Beach, January"

*Gettysburg Review:* "A Cardinal In Connecticut"

*Gulf Stream:* "Ginny's Best Seafood Shack, Zanesville, Ohio"

*Harpur Palate:* "Final Road Trip, West Virginia," "Multiple Choice Test," "The Bride, December"

*Midwest Quarterly Review:* "Deer Photography"

*Minnesota Review:* "Mammals, Late November"

*New Ohio Review:* "A Swallow in May, Northern Michigan," (under the title "Yesterday in Northern Michigan"), "Cedar Waxwing, Late November"

*Sky Island Journal:* "Violin Concerto"

*Tar River Poetry:* "Baba Murders the Cheese"

*Terrain.org:* "The Bob & Mary Diner, New Buffalo, Ohio, 2008," "The New Neighbor," "Fabio and the Animals"

*Valparaiso Poetry Review:* "Pelican," "What Gander Knows"

# CONTENTS

PART TWO: BEAUTIFUL CLOWNS

PART THREE:   HOME BEFORE DARK

*For Anne*

PART ONE:  SMALL

# NIGHT SKY, ATLANTIC COAST

Like a child, I look up till my neck hurts.
In the black sky, four planes float,
two large, two small, blinking
red and silver, toys of physics
held aloft by mystical threads,
a vacuum, a nothing that's less than air.

Is there a saint or two on board?
Or a child? Is there some wonder
up there among the hustlers,
the busy carriers of loss?
They talk too much and count all day,
measuring. They eat magic
and chew with their mouths open,
riding along in a performance
so far away I almost believe
they like being small.

## VOLUNTEER FIRE DEPARTMENT,
## SOUTHEASTERN OHIO

I don't expect enchantment here
in my mother's back yard—August,
fading green, hot evening breeze, some birdsong.
I'm her Detroit visitor, fifty-four, trying to read
while she plays cards in town, a mile away.

Up the hill, a woman in her garden
faces me as she hunches to her beans.
I feel watched, as I always did here.

And then the sirens start—a slow, bass growl
rising to a squeal, three long calls to the men:
quit supper, rush to the station, climb on.

Long before the interstate,
boys sat on the drugstore steps,
reading aloud the states on license plates
as cars and downshifting semis
groaned into the turn at Elm and Dexter.

We recited the states as if they were movies or wishes.
The Tennessee plate was shaped like Tennessee,
a long horizontal with wriggling vertical edges
for rivers. White digits on black.

We ate licorice, chewed pink gum,
traipsed downhill in gravel alleys
from school to the flat town square.

Coming upon an empty pack of Lucky Strikes,
we fought to be the one to stomp it,
punch a buddy's arm and yell *Lucky on me!*
The socked boy must never cry,
though Wayne Poulton did once.

The sirens grow quicker, more shrill.
A half-mile over, trucks roar down old 21,
once an important road, winding
through the ordinary town.

The whirling lights cross the rickety bridge
over Duck Creek, and in the flood plain's pasture
nervous cows trot to the far fence.
The birds have shushed.

My mother would know the gardening woman
who peers out from under her floppy hat.
Chances are, I'm supposed to know her too.

Once the sirens are gone, the birds return,
and I glance uphill to see if she's still peeking.
We are each other's newest intrusions,
and each of us waits for the other to say,
*Somebody's in trouble. Somebody's on fire.*

# THE BRIDE, DECEMBER

Parked at a curb, I watch that slender beauty
carrying one small girl
and holding the hand of another,
all three in white. She hurries
and leans a little forward, like an athlete.

What's she doing outside the church?
It's no rehearsal—she's in her gown,
and they are three white shapes
quickening in the cold, no snow

against the courtyard cobblestone
along the church's limestone wall,
under a low gray winter sky.

She's forgotten something—her coin purse,
I suppose, or the baby's binky. Yet
she's calm at first as she tries the side door.
The honey-stained wood looks warm as amber.

She releases the older girl to let her left hand
palm the black iron hinges,
while her right grips the curved latch.
She yanks twice. Nothing gives,
and time is starting to matter.

She doesn't know I wanted to help,
had thought of stepping into the cold to offer.
But I'm an old man in an old car.
Had I been lurking? Was I peculiar?

She's disappeared around the corner,
the steps of a dancer, silent and light,
or a thief running off with answers.
The little girls will remember none of this.

## MAMMALS, LATE NOVEMBER

Science promised a blue sky,
but it's locked up somewhere, four days now,
prisoner in a far cave.

We mammals shuffle about,
making leaves make noise,
the squirrels and I. *Whisk whisk*
go the dry, cold leaves,

and I keep turning to see who's there,
following me in the fallen landscape.
A silent hawk dives, grabs a mouse,
pulls him high above the brown.

The ceramic sky sinks a little more,
spitting flurries that fall and light
on the tongues of teen girls gliding
and bouncing along brick sidewalks
toward the school, the gym,

where indecent, lithe boys
with absurd, nascent whiskers,
sweat with a basketball, whirling
as if they've never heard of weather.
Weather is one more story grandmothers tell.
The boys wink at it,

for they are lathered like ponies,
hard as beach rocks—cold day, hot gym,

they bump each other and lean
into weather and time, preparing,

in case the stories are true after all.
But they don't know that's what they're doing.
They don't know anything.

# THE BOB AND MARY CAFE, NEW BUFFALO, OHIO 2008
*Every succulent sandwich under $4.99*

A summer Thursday and Roger Dowell
in overalls and long grey beard sits
hunched at the counter, the village at his back
and, farther off, the long-dead coal field.

For $3.99 the special: fried baloney on grilled white,
home fries, sizzling strips of pepper and onion.
He likes the smells, takes his time,

stares now and then into the kitchen,
where Mary glances toward him
and mumbles something to Janie, her cook.

Whatever Mary said, Roger hears *so sad.*
And *odd?* He's pretty sure. So he digs
in his pocket, finds four wadded bills
to smack on the Formica, wets his napkin,

wipes his fingers and the butter knife,
half-mumbles, half-growls something—
nothing you could call a word—
at nothing Mary knows she said.

He takes a dozen careful steps toward the door,
pauses there, points the dull blade at his ear,
moves it in circles. Against their will, people look.

His daughter's little house sits two miles north,
near the old Walhonding Mine and Tunnel Hill.
She worries about her father, and debt, and sinkholes,
which the deep coal shafts might have left a century ago.

He heads away from town on the gravel berm,
patches of goldenrod beside him now and then,
and cattails, and some asters, purple and white.
He walks on the left, facing traffic,
as he was taught to do so long ago.

# GINNY'S BEST SEAFOOD SHACK, ZANESVILLE, OHIO

In this stiff booth, how can I soothe
my sobbing mother, who insisted
we come here—cheesecake for her,
beer-battered shrimp for me.
We've earned it, she said, the day after
the end of my father's long dying.

In his hospice room, she slept
four months on a cot.
On the phone yesterday
she told a one-year widow friend,
"Your Dan was easier—he went so fast."

This morning she cleared my father's closet
and called Goodwill, then had me drive her
with the revolver to the pawnbroker,
who gave us three dollars for the gun's bones—
my father had tossed the cylinder
when she offered to kill them both.

2:30 now—only three other diners at Ginny's,
but they've noticed our drama
and complain with their eyes.
I'm supposed to *do* something.

Who can blame them on this sunny
October workday? They came for
the creamy linguini, the key lime pie.

# THE NEW NEIGHBOR

You know this man, or dozens of him:
lives alone, speaks so little, such grudging
helloes, that I wonder if words to him

are underwater sounds, the claims
of the drowning, or mumbled prayers,
or rattling items in forgotten drawers.

Fifty-something, he's a lean silence,
hands on hips, studying some storm
that he alone perceives, as men replace

the siding on his suburban bungalow.
This good labor wastes nothing, and I'm sure
he searched hard, paid cash, did not negotiate.

In his driveway, the oversized pickup sits,
white as a bride. He's modified the muffler
to feel the rumble of an engine's speech,

sounds he heard in youth, like me, I'd guess,
on thin, dark roads, where nights of roar
and thumping songs were louder

than the plaintive notes he silently preferred.
From a nearby orchard, he learned the smell
of peaches, which he never meant to memorize.

# THREE EGGS, FLORIDA BEACH, JANUARY

Oval as an egg, topped by a swatch of white hair,
an old man on the sand, in a drizzle,
turns to his fat blond cocker:
*Lady! Are you coming?*
His steps are even smaller than mine,
so Lady could keep the pace,
but she's sitting, sniffing, staring out to sea,
not at all sure about this foggy walk.


I'm cheap, and this morning I'm proud
to be wearing a three-dollar belt
from the secondhand clothing store.
There's a groove at the notch
where a dead man buckled my belt.
I use the same hole. Imagine: a dead man
just my size in the middle, a third egg.

I've been thinking of getting another dog.
I wouldn't pump her up like Lady,
but I'd spoil her some.
She'd sleep in my bed; there'd be long talks.
Watching the news, I'd lie on thick carpet
to stretch my back and share
the cocker perspective—even a dog
who quivers when trucks or thunder
grumble by and shake our leafy trees.

Without Lady, that old man might
never exit his condo or unlock the hands

he carries behind him. He tugs the leash,
and they inch along, heads down,
leaning into January mist. Sometimes,
even in Florida, the wind whips sand
across your ankles and into your eyes.

# DOG THOUGHTS

What if my speckled dog
who loped six years in the meadow
now sat in a rocker, staring
at books, for hours, or TV's news,
practiced all the bright morning,
or cook shows, cop shows, show shows,
and even sports?
What if my speckled dog
gazed out the grey window
and twice a day
woofed his deep thoughts
to the empty street?
Or whined longingly
to the yellow Lab trotting by
on the far side of the glass?
What if I had a dog?

# THE WIDOWER'S RAT

In November a rat appeared out back,
among the seeds my birds and squirrels
had spilled from feeders.
The rat held the bits in his front paws,
as if to study them, or pray.

Every morning, along with doves and sparrows,
the rat kept coming. At first light
I'd look twice to be sure
the gray scooting thing
wasn't a bird, maybe a junco,
head and back the color of slate
the belly a lighter gray or creamy white.

I've always liked the junco's lively hop
and the way he kicks at seeds
to pop them out of the grass.
His eyes are shiny black beads,
and when he flies, white tail feathers
flash out from under the gray.

And what about the cardinal couple,
sharing food, beak to beak?
Sometimes one stands guard on a branch
while the other pecks in the grass.
Across the trees, he sings his need to her.

Soon enough the rat brought family.
They nested in the shed with the cobwebs.

With winter inching in, they planned
to trick the cold.

The rats were here to stay, it seemed.
The birds began to peck each other.
The sparrows were the worst.

Doves are oafs, but one confronted the rat,
raised one wing—shield or weapon or both—
then charged him in a waddle.
The rat looked amused.

Soon enough the juncos and others
snuck off to other yards—or headed south.
I considered a winter without birds.

Saturday a rat baby found his way
into the recycling bin, then couldn't flee
the blue plastic cave, squealed on and on
and on, till I put the shovel to him—
squeal and whack, once,
squeal and whack, twice, and more,
sometimes the belly, sometimes the neck.

Twice I missed and wondered if the rats
were grinning at me. They might—
they weren't grieving. Rats don't grieve.
Plenty of babies where that one came from.

I laid the corpse at the base of the feeder pole,
to see if his father returned to eat him like cheese,
finish all but the head, then slink away.

After three days, something had chewed up
all but the largest baby bones,
and the flesh from the skull was gone,
even the little round ears,
and of course the core and the legs—
day by day more pieces gone.

After a week the rats had disappeared.
Did they grieve that baby after all?
Did my poison get some? In any case

I had my quiet back,
and most of the missing returned—
the thick, plodding doves, a dozen sparrows,
even the high-kicking juncos, beautiful clowns,
who seemed again at peace, and of course
the squirrels, who never left.

# A FLOCK OF STARLINGS FORMS

*More than 95 percent of the nestling's food is animal matter.*
(Jackie Collins, *Starling Talk*)

In order to forget descending winter's grey
weight crawling over my shoulders and pressing
down my back, I was inhaling poems,
little rectangles, like my suburban bungalow,

when a massive starling squeal
thickened in the window I'd cracked for air.
Across the street I saw the mass
of their bluish sheen with creamy dots,
heard the clatter of their fellowship
as they debated whether to honor
or mock my boundary and tidy bib
of yard out back.

If I fall down dead in nature, dead weight
like a rolled bale of hay in a sunset field,
a swarm of speckled them will dine on me—

dozens of birds screaming, quarreling
for space at the table of me. They'd eat
me minced with beetles, a casserole
with worms and bits of corn. That is why
I stay indoors. That is why I read.

# THE GENEROUS MARSH OF ME

Let me be acres of high grass
absorbing the May swamp
in a cattail way, redwings
landing in the generous marsh of me.

Let small birds make a breeze
a foot or two above me, fluttering
across my chest, or even landing there.
They seem light as moths, and their claws
don't hurt when they squeeze
the reeds of me, clinging in wind.

I'll be the dank host the heron
steps across. He lifts his slow, bony legs
and his feet skim the lily pads

atop the muck of my left shoulder,
my right knee. It tickles, though pieces of me
drift, dissolve and sink. I shred.

The heron moves in a cautious,
weary way, monkish, bluish prophet,
his neck a holy rope, coiled—till it
springs the beak that flashes.

The indifferent carp are deadly slow.
Pay attention, fish. A plodding bird-bulk
looms, a hairy spy with a lightning blade.

I'm the mud witness, and this is where I lie,
a congregation of one in the hall of mayhem,
dark water, where herons slaughter fish
among green reeds that lightly sway.

# MULTIPLE CHOICE TEST

At fifty-two, she's crashed her car
in a grey suburb north of Detroit.

She climbs in her long cloth coat
up from a ditch toward the freeway's edge,

but somewhere in her rising, she slips,
and strands of weeds stick to her left sleeve

as she waves her arms over her head.
Her face is nothing but wide eyes

and a small, dark, oval mouth,
which seems stuck open forever

to say *O!* and nothing else. She needs
to tell her story, how only a moment ago,

she was soaring, though she hadn't meant to.
Something pulled her and she flew a few moments

toward space. But all that thrill and wonder
have shrunk to a fundamental *O!* –

like a blackened mark on an answer sheet.
Her skull has sopped all the knowledge

it can handle: speed, roar of traffic, wind, soot.
Her nose and mouth are filling with carbon,

and she knows she can never utter what flying was like—
floating off the planet, no pilot, no rules,

then the slam of metal into mud,
the whack of answer, flat, unambiguous,

an absence of echo and every gentle thing.
Yet she seems unharmed, and climbs

where instinct points, toward the traffic, the noise.
She clutches at cattails and weeds on her

dreamy way up. What a tale she could tell,
if she had words to paint her rising—
this miracle, this lucky girl.

# FLIGHT

Last week I was six miles up,
sitting in cold blue, above a mess
of March clouds, strewn like ruffled rugs—
whites, grays, shreds—and under those,

a drizzle, I suppose, and everyone down there
agreeing they needed rain, people glad
about the pitter, or diner chatter, or Sunday nap,

and the rich plains soaking. I actually began
to like flying, feeling alone and removed.
Then my glance caught the wing quivering—

an absolutely normal thing, I knew,
that silver tremble of negotiation,
a dialogue with air—but a lot more air
than slice of wing to ride it. I tried

to wink it away, to be a child, dressing
in puffy layers for some special, unfamiliar cold—
because I'd seen some simple physics happen.

Now I link that shivering wing
to a pine tree's punch-drunk bend and wobble,
its March sparrows squeezing harder,
little talons in spitting snow. In such conceits

I'm quite a linker of things as I grow
a few more metaphors removed
from ice or the rocks ice splits.

I build the bit of distance words can make
against what's raw. Remove,
and then remove again. Never trust
a March that's blue—sparrows don't.

I wrap the quilted layers thick around me
and feel my coiled toes hanging on.
I peep to strangers in the rain, as they
fall away and spin, farther off and small.

# SCHENECTADY

Mid-September, already a brown leaf,
and six finches squabble for thistle,
a ruckus, a squeal for pecking order.

Suddenly they're still as stone.
They sense a shadow, a whiff of trouble
hovering over their squeaky song.
And they're gone.

Last night I dreamed I was trapped
in Schenectady in an elevator
falling in dark sky, pitched in all directions,

and me in that old-timey cage, accordion gate,
black iron frame and bars, brass trim,
some 1952 department store, vast as night.

My vessel drifted, then sped, grew nimble,
dodging black holes—though I could feel the pull.

I've never been to Schenectady.
I love the name, but what about the falling?

And all those store customers, loud, jostling,
talk talk talk, Dutch, African, Italian, Mohawk,
American jabberwockies, getting and spending
and uttering—gathered humans, murmur and mayhem.

I woke sweating, grabbing at air—

though the elevator's iron should have held,
and the tufted red bench was padded.

I could catch my breath, could tilt the cage,
a miracle, to pivot and steer, away
from black holes and raptors—

if only I could match the finch's
yellow ease as he dips and rises.

But I don't want to be a bird—
mites and lice, a cat around every corner,
the endless labor for flecks of seed,
little wings beating, a frenzy . . . .

Yet I do admire the landings, graceful,
focused on food or branch, effortless, it seems.
And look how they quit their giddy chatter
at the shadow of a hawk.

# GWEN IN MANHATTAN, A LOVE STORY

*Against all odds,*
*Honey, we're the big door prize.*

                        *--John Prine*


I need to believe in Gwen across the way,
the twelfth-floor office window, her flowing hair,
modest smile despite the bills, files, and Penelope
three feet away, chomping on her gum.

Gwen waters the plant on her desk.
I'd guess her voice is sing-song,
eager to please. She'll need to
learn some husky, cool aplomb
if she's to rise to the executive suites

where, six floors up, her lover Ken
(I named him Ken), short and wiry,
flips a yoyo, makes it walk the dog,
tosses tennis balls at a waste basket—
he's fidgety, a small white monkey,
unibrow, bug eyes—he swings on vines
and chatters, a clown with nothing to say.
He sells annuities; he wears you down.
In spite of himself, he prospers.

Gwen is his only elegant thing.
He sends her pastel cards with gauzy figures,
tells her she's his sky, his butterfly,
his only friend, and she thinks it might be true,
She grew up in Elmira; she wants to believe it all.

# BABA MURDERS THE CHEESE

Wednesday. I've just begun to slice
a hard, salty sheep's milk cheese

to coat my gut for beer and whiskey,
wedges against the winter dusk.

I run hot water on the blade so it'll glide,
but my teeth stay clenched,

and I grip the knife handle
as if I want to wring its neck.

Again my rooms are looking at me.
Am I slouching? Shuffling

through the little house? Wallowing
in the old, trite questions?

I consider recording a week of myself.
But I'd have to pause on Thursdays

when my daughter's daughter,
two years a human, swaggers in

like the sailor-sot in the jolly song—
*What do you say to a drunken toddler,*

*What do you say to a drunken toddler,*
*earl-aye in the moor-ning?*

She calls me *Baba*—neither holy man nor father,
but the *Baba* she's wrung from *Grandpa.*

I don't know why she's glad to be here,
but she marches in and heads for noise—

drum the ottoman, pound the leather, strum
the kiddie banjo, shake the diapered rump.

Then stack the blocks. High. No, higher,
into thin air. Her lower lip creeps out,

covers the upper, and her tongue
sneaks from the corner of her mouth,

the grin of the hyper-focused, the grin
of the wicked. She knows the big joy's coming,

the swipe, the crash, the roar of color and action,
an even taller tower underway in seconds.

Thursdays are hers. My splendid,
tortured Wednesday questions vanish

and hide in the baseboards like shamed mice.
Maybe I could drop a piece of magical cheese

to lure them back, but I know
they won't come out from the gloom they love
till the boogie-woogie girl goes home.

# ADORATION ON THE BEACH, JANUARY

Here on the balcony, with binoculars, I love
the dozen early humans out there on the beach,
standing in cold wind to adore the sun's rising
over a trawler on the horizon.

I'm besotted with the notion I'd see Morocco
if I could squint that hard. But a magic
I might believe is that pair of backlit lovers
sitting on a dune, silhouetted sculptures.

His hoodie's top is pointed, and his legs
spread in a V to make a place for her
with his arms draped over her shoulders.

Her hair's pulled up into a mussed ball,
and she keeps pushing her glasses to her brow.
Now she turns her face north into the winter chill
and I wonder if she's begging the wind to relax.

As she looks back out to sea, she suddenly
reaches skyward and claps her hands at the sun,
coaxing him to hoist his big self up.

She cheers the sun the way she'd call her dog—
with applause, a cookie, a voice full of love,
as if the dog's return at dusk
is all she'll ever ask of anything.

# VIOLIN CONCERTO

The soloist is a pretty redhead
with a tomboy's freckled face.
But she's stern, as if the music
is summer labor—wood or hay to gather.

She wrestles the score to swelling,
then tenderness, then staccato. Her hands
jerk and her fingers quiver like bees aroused.
The pinky slides, skids to a scream,
high and alone, trembles for a half note
and moves on, a wren that blinked.

Her hair's a tight bun,
shoulders muscular, carved,
sinew and vein in the neck
and a taut core. She is music's soldier
and leans with the demands, sways, then
yanks herself away, as if from stench.
She sweats a little, working
for one right move after another—
each move's an answer.

She's an old soul, earnest and sad,
laboring, a girl in a lake, trying to rise
through thick, complacent water,
pulling herself up and up

till she shatters the surface,
and with open arms
hugs the whole blue sky,

inhales—dramatic, almost a violence—
and opens her eyes
to the vast woods around the lake.
Treading water, she calls
for the animals, and they come.

# FINAL ROAD TRIP, WEST VIRGINIA

Blinded by cancer, my wife asks me
what she's missing along these rises
and curves from Buckannon to Ripley.

I don't mention diesel or dump trucks
or hills gouged for coal—facts and myths

hovering like vultures about to descend
and feed. The road cuts mountains

and glides along creeks and valleys
where wind and water have eaten rock.

Bound tight for centuries, mineral walls
seem to part for us, just now, *today*, releasing

a big, slow breath of light that pours upon
more green than turning earth deserves.

Shall I tell a dying skeptic I could swear I see
the shoulder of a god, bent and tending

luscious, ragged fields, abandoned land
transformed to meadows with dotted gold?

Long-haired girls recline there, their pioneer
skirts flowing in sun, as pasture stones

dissolve in dew and flood
and wild grasses lean in the breeze.

PART TWO:  BEAUTIFUL CLOWNS

# FABIO AND THE ANIMALS

Blue skies last Thursday along the trail
where a cardinal couple, ten feet up a pine,
fed each other, one seed at a time.

A few yards later a different cardinal
lay in dirt, a hawk-shredded corpse,
feathers scattered, while in the budding treetops
the first pair fluted their red love.

In another quarter mile I nearly
stepped on a pair of garter snakes
coiled around each other, writhing
under midday sun. They paused,
raised their heads to scan me
as I hovered over their sex,
which looked like war.

But today's a lazy, gray Sunday for coffee,
YouTube, and Portugal where Fabio, age four,
declines some bites of octopus
his mother's cut for lunch.

He's firm. He wants his animals *alive!*
Wants them *standing up!*
He raises his hands like a conductor.

Off camera, his mother's voice
sounds adoring, even teary, as she
grants a lunch of noodles and potatoes,
the souls of which Fabio has not pondered.

But on this dewy morning he makes me
reconsider immortal greens, pasta, beans.
Then I recall the octopus's serpent legs
surging with murderous speed and grace.
He pries little creatures from the rocks,
choosing the tasty ones
to crush with his beak, and gobble,

whether or not each shrimp, crab,
or tiny fish has finished his sentence
in an ocean so dark and silent
no one knows just what to say.

# WHITE PINE, FEBRUARY

Out back yesterday a pine branch snapped
under snow and ice. It *cracked*, dropped fast,
a rumble, hiss and whisper
of cones and twigs on rooftop shingles.

The branch, maybe ten feet long,
looks peaceful, even elegant, on the ground
under rising mounds of snow
that begin to resemble white animals—
turtles and groundhogs, or the squirrels
that crawled and scooted on that branch.
Squirrels are riff raff, but they seemed
always on a skyward route, up and up,
quick and reckless, flying rats.
They leapt among the branches
and clung there, nested there.

When I was fourteen, I rode out with my father
to Uncle Ray's farm, and we shot three grays,
brought them home to skin and gut
on the work bench in the garage.
My mother fried the pieces like sausage,
with green peppers and onions,
but we could hardly cut the flesh,
much less chew it. And I remembered
what the meat had been that morning.

Who did we think we were? Pioneers?
My father was no farm kid—a town boy,

he grew up with pavement and plumbing,
was only as tough as he needed to be.

And I was a kid who thought of trees
as skyward avenues. I wondered
what rites might suit squirrels,
what mix of sand and clay might
hold them down where they belonged.

# CEDAR WAXWING, LATE NOVEMBER

In the crook of a bare maple branch
a lone cedar waxwing sits. I thought they
went south, but not all, I guess, or not yet.

There are big blue holes in the clouds today
and only a moderate chill, a day to be sociable—
and waxwings tend toward groups.

But there he sits, no berry calling him,
nor women, nor daring flights among thickets.
His high-pitched note is mute.

The breast of the cedar waxwing looks softer
than anything I've seen. No one's discerned
a single feather etched in the fuzz

of his tan-gold-grey. That black mask
is a clown's toy, dandy more than bandit.
Small orange beads dangle on his wingtips,

and look how the buff-grey tail concludes
in black and lemony stripes. But what good
is all that art on the eve of winter, this bird left

with his choice to stay put, and only me
to impress? I've heard that waxwings in courtship
pass fruit and bugs back and forth. They dance

and finish with a gentle touching of beaks.
Maybe my lone bird is lookout for his tribe,

or decoy—an offering to any hawk he can't deceive.

December's shouldering in, and here we are,
me wondering, him staring. His feathers fluff
in a bit of wind. Some twigs fall. We see each other.

# A SWALLOW IN MAY, NORTHERN MICHIGAN

Four times today that bee has banged
his head against my window.
He wants erotic pollen and thinks
he smells it here, the indoor side of glass.

These days people say madness
is expecting something new
from old behavior. So this must be
a lunatic bee—bad wiring or bad parents,
the bad apple, the not-our-kind-of
bee. In the corner of my eye,
like a floater, but more sudden,
he breaks left and attacks the window,
throbbing with what he must have.
pounding with *I love this, I want that.*

Yesterday in northern Michigan the blue sky
unzipped itself and let a swallow fall, fast,
beak first, so straight it seemed
he'd aimed for asphalt—saw a bug there,
had to have it. The bird bounced once,
twenty yards ahead. I had to steer
a little left to clear the body.

This May's been cool and wet, such a daily, fresh
dawn breath that the season and the trees
did not expect it. Only crazy animals *expect,*

like bees, or a swallow lit gold in morning sun,
heading for his usual spot on a white pine branch
only two lanes east, where the world was
what he remembered and desired.

# HEMLOCK, FINCH, OCTOBER

*In English, 'hemlock' refers not only to poison hemlock, but to water hemlock,*
*hemlock water dropwort, lesser hemlock (fool's parsley), and other herbs as well,*
*all resembling each other in their lacy, umbrella-like flowers and tiny fruits.*
(Enid Bloch)

Here on the trail is a poison hemlock plant.
Over there is a hemlock tree, its elegant skirts
unfurled. Know your hemlocks.

Notice the stalks of milkweed too, soft
and oddly erotic, autumn's dirty white
gazing down a slope dotted mustard-gold.

And now willow, holly berry, bramble bush,
and by the creek a pumpkin, possum-gnawed,
which reminds me of the dead finch

back at the house, under the window. I'm here
to forget her, lying there, her downy back that familiar
olive-dun, nothing noteworthy except for death,

until I was startled by her eyes, squeezed shut,
a scrupulous child counting time in hide and seek.
Ready or not, here comes the world's big puzzle

to kill the finch, tell her *A*, then tell her *B*,
then gloat that  *C*  was the answer all along,
and how could she be so slow? Look out,

little bird. In that window, you only think you see
some airy square of blue—backdrop
for yellow trees and a thousand places to land.

# WHAT GANDER KNOWS

After winter, before spring, the shore's
surviving, upright pines and maples
are backdrop for a single leaning birch,
ghostly white hypotenuse that wrinkles

and wobbles in the lake, which interprets
everything. Gander sees his reflection there,
brown as the curve of his big brown back
trimmed in black and cream.

His long neck is a question mark
though the hook of his head holds confident eyes,
which see a bounty in the water's mirror—
clouds, brush, self, brood, and the plenty below.

He thinks he's been nominated for something,
and he's glad to know the rippling trees and he
are fellow souls, though the animal in him
fouls the paths he swaggers through.

Already the sky's forgotten him, his clan, the loud
scar they cut across the blue just minutes ago.
Their honking bluster's quiet now. Gravity
has briefly tamed the ragged arrow of geese,

shrunk them all to makers of a bubbly wake.
A triangle flows from their rumps, as they follow
high-headed Gander's steady line,
their answer barge, easing across the muddy lake.

# A PELICAN TALE

i

Next life I'll be a fine, wise pelican,
slow-bobbing on dreamy waves that heave
and roll like hips and shoulders under a sky.

I'll be ugly in a Jurassic way—
none of this was my fault.

I'll know fleas and mites, hurricanes
and fishing nets, but such an ease of gliding

over water, forty miles an hour, scouring
the sea's abundance—and then

to climb the sky, to peak, dip a wing
and pivot, collapse into a blade, and dive!
*Smack* the water! Split the sea!

My white wake sprays
as I scoop a flounder up.

I perch on rails and posts—
my agnostic grin and poker player's eyes,
my feathered, endless throat.

ii

Then again, as pelican, I'd have an uncle
who bit off more than he could chew

and some scaly thing flopped in his pouch,
wriggled in his neck, crawled back
almost to light, its nerves on fire.

The item made such a nuisance of itself
that Uncle P just quit, bore the shiny fish
in a lumbering climb to the top of blue,

twisted upside-down, belly to the sun,
and spit his burden back to the sea,

as if humiliating the fish
had always been the plan.

He concluded with a graceful dive
and mediocre splash, failing
with a touch of style, trying

to save face. In the pelican business
reputation is everything,
and he knew we'd seen the truth.

My uncle fled. We've heard he lives alone
up the Carolina coast, where the nights
can be unkindly cold and full of shame.

# PELICAN

Six pelicans crossing blue sky
surprise me, each pair of wings rising
and falling at angles unlike the others,
as if to row their skiff across the air,
all those eyes scanning the sea.

Then they're lower, and the dark wings
flatten for coasting—the harmony!—
at forty miles an hour,
a child's height above the water.

They find a rail, hover a moment,
and land light as moths in a June breeze,
tiptoe dancers, pelican pirouettes,
except for two off-balance clowns
pounding at air as if the planet had jerked.

On the bait shop's dock they sit and grin,
seven pounds apiece. Their cores
are boulders in some ancient myth,
and gray feathers, etched in rows
of slight curves, could be a script.
Who combed those lines?
What language is it?

The eyes neither stare nor look away
as the beak's long blade tucks itself
against the sheath of neck. Pelican
gets some joke and isn't sharing.

He isn't leaving either.
He knows the ocean's full of food,
and he's especially confident today.
What he holds in his pouch
squirms. He waits. He's got all day.

# GULLS

Monday I watched a Laughing Gull
work an hour to shred a fish
too big to gulp. Wednesday
a Ring-Billed Gull caught a crab,
dropped it, grabbed it up, swallowed,
struggled to govern the thing
that wriggled in his white throat.

At the beach today, somebody's grandson,
about eight, skinny red-head,
holds a bag of bread chunks.
He extends his arm, opens his palm,
thinks twice, retreats toward
the paunchy grandpa with a camera,
turns again to the sea and reaches out again
and again until he's failed three times to feed the birds.

Now, over the Atlantic, gulls circle a spot.
They look casual out there. Are they bored,
drifting and scanning, so many fish in the sea?
And time's only starting to crawl toward dusk.

At the pier's end, five fishermen
lean over the ocean. Above them,
eight gulls gather on a lamp post.
Books say gulls are gregarious,
might mate for life and some colonies
shun runaway parents.

Are there philosopher gulls,
bogged down with what they know
about that first layer of light
beneath the ocean's skin?
Do they wonder why simpleton fish
don't simply swim deeper down?

There goes a pair speeding across the sky—
They don't wonder.

A half-dozen others spiral lazily up,
coast awhile—maybe they're the thinkers.
No. One by one, they peel off
and dive. Six white splashes pock the sea.

I try to care about fish. I try
to demonize the gull's beak,
hooked tip, efficient weapon.

Here comes that same freckled boy,
this time with a larder of whole grain chips.
He looks out to the looping birds.

When they smack the water
in white explosions, the child
asks his ruddy grandpa
if the birds are killing themselves.

The old man laughs—too hard.
*The birds are fine,* he says.
*Hold it out again! All the way!*

He means to be jolly,
but these are commands.

The gulls swarm, close and wild.
The boy stands his ground.
Grandpa says, *That's it! Do it again!*
and the picture-snapping begins.

# DEER PHOTOGRAPHY

On my laptop, the doe in shade was dark
and unromantic, so I withdrew some shadow
from her face and flanks. That turned her
grey in late May—and the ground too,
and the trees and their deep leaves
from November half a year ago, all grey.

Later, in a magazine, I came across the label
*rat-grey fungus*, words so right I forgot
the doe and remembered last September's
backyard rat. I got three shots of him—
the exterminators might need to know, *this*
kind of rat. There must be many kinds. My rat

ate fallen birdseed under the feeders.
The fidgety birds, the reckless squirrels, and the rat
ignored each other—kicked seed around
and fed side by side, like children's
parallel play in a sandbox.

But each dove raised one wing
against the rat if he came near, as if
to shield itself against what's hideous.
Or maybe the dove thought his wing
would menace the rat, or shun it,
make it feel bad about itself and go away.

The rat munched on, no need for allies,
though the book says rats are *sociable*

and some humans make them pets,
train them, name them.

I began to think of other long-faced mammals—
horse, donkey, weasel, possum, fox,
elegant collie dog. Then rat again.

I told myself the grey I gave the doe
was spiritual: she became a mist
removed from garish color and appetite
as she chewed on leafy trees of grey,
turned her mulish face toward me, ears up,
and fixed me in her big black eyes.

# A CARDINAL IN CONNECTICUT

My daughter, thirty, calls from New Haven,
the maple-filled park that flanks her building.
She's walking her wild young dog,
the world's only bad yellow Lab,
who barks once to verify he's there.
She's strong, a runner,
but he yanks her. I've seen it.

The other day, she says,
a bee approached her bearded date,
and he seized up, flailing and yelping like opera
till he fell down, rolled like a man afire,
arose, sprinted fifty yards ahead, kept going.
Another man never laughed.
Another texted with his ex during dessert.

My daughter's boss gives a lot of orders.
Don't bother him with ideas. Last month
Human Resources shorted her pay. Twice.

Last night, lots of lightning there.
Across the street, a house caught fire,
her first vision of a home in flames.

A cardinal trills over the phone,
testifying from Connecticut to Detroit.
The dog barks again, wants her
to hang up. I interrupt to ask
if she's hearing her cardinal.

She laughs, calls me Bird Nerd, then sees
the old man whose house burned down.
In his yard he's staring at the rubble.
She decides to walk over, see if she can help.

There goes the cardinal again,
and a deep bark from the dog.

I've been with her in that park
and I can see the bird there,
red center of everything, pulling
a hundred branches into himself,

the singing hub of a shaggy circle,
my daughter, her dog, the old man,
the acres of brush and trees around them.

## SPARROW SHADOW

Morning sun on a sparrow's flight
creates a shadow, scooting along,
bird on grass, gray on green,
large and fuzzy as a heron, and fast.

The shadow's a matter of light,
waves and absence, not soul, not ghost.

Now the sparrow's gone—just like that!
The shadow too. They are not dead yet,
though the bird will dissolve someday
into other matter.

But what becomes of the shadow,
which surely one could measure?
It must be as real as the bird.

Maybe the shadow will only disappear,
not cease—a phantom's trick after all.

The bird has the integrity to die
and see what else. The shadow—sneaky,
safe and certain as an echo—roosts
in the Great Rookery of Shadows,
wherever that may be.

LANDSCAPE: HOME BEFORE DARK

# HILLS

In March the hills gaze down
at the brown Ohio—the barge, the tug,
the train tracks, two-lanes bending
and straightening, fat, black cones of coal,
private munching and breeding
of muskrats. Snakes and bats.
Yellow flash of finch.
Yodeling catbird. Moths.

The hills know beauty and minor lives
are all they've got. They lean
with the brown weight of hearing themselves.

Except for winter, I wouldn't mind
having a roadside stand halfway up a hill.
I'd sell boiled peanuts from Georgia,
fossils and beaver teeth,
as branches cracked above me
with hungry deer tramping
along supper paths they've forged.

I wonder how anyone could fail to love the hills.
They've listened for a long time to the way
the sky seems always about to speak,
always some big announcement.

So the hills ripple and stretch
to send their chatter out
to interrupt the sky,
which has been too vast, too long.
The hills have had about enough.

# THE OLD MAN AND THE DAMSELFLY

Who can tell a dragonfly from a damselfly
in the rich green shade?
The silky, whimsical flight is a small chaos,
blues and greens and purples frail and gorgeous
as they rest on fallen wood in a stream.
Damselflies live half a year or more.

The deep grooves in the sugar maple's bark
are quiet, like human skin aging.
Weren't we put here to be a noise?
I hear more noise than I make.
I think I hear more noise than others do.
Sometimes wind makes big trees moan
as they sway and try to lie down.

In the swamp an April redwing croaks
disapproval from his perch on a cattail.
But he can trill like a flute too, or
scream at the sky till his red shoulders
quiver. In juicy spring, he dives at you,
tells you how rugged he is,
how brilliant, and lonely,
amid the jittery flight of bugs.

# LEAF ON A LAKE

On the water a leaf twitches in wind.
At first it's a turtle's head,
or a snake, sliding east, then west,
back and forth, urgent, hungry.

No, just a leaf, no monster, no myth.
Sometimes it pauses, becomes
a shuddering fleck, then a hand,
a torn page ripped from home, scooting
left and right in a straight line,
a child in a game—sprint
to the totem, gallop back to base.

Chatting people saunter by. It's Sunday.

For the sake of magic, I almost wish
the leaf were turtle or snake.
(Now it's a frog's webbed foot! Detached,
it flutters upon the indifferent lake,
which only wants a nap).

One wet leaf on a lake in a breeze
should not behave like that.
It has no standing here.
Surely some underwater engine
shoves the fast, hapless self
into mindless dashes back and forth.
Surely some unloved bulk of current
is the force, slow, but so willful

even the water is drowning
(and more desperate than wind).

Yet the leaf seems happy enough,
out of breath but perky, dancing a jig,
clapping its hands over its head.
It's a leaf, and it's waving to shore.

# DROUGHT, AUGUST

Even dawn is a weight, too warm,
but the sparrows talk a little
as they scratch in the brown yard,
and up in the maple two squirrels
jabber and harass each other.

A quarter mile south, the creek is dry,
its great blue heron gone.
Soon the heat of morning
will burn away the dew.

But a faint breeze breathes now and then:
leaves quiver, and small birds
make tiny song. A bee and two moths
are busy in the shaft of light
coloring everything pale amber,

and the sky turns to gold
the crow flying over
with breakfast in its beak.

## SPARROWS

Early April. My four-foot hedge at dawn
dulls beneath a crust of snow, needles
so dark they're hardly green at all.

The middle's a mess of twig-to-twig
contradictions, sharp slivers, caves of shadow
where a sparrow couple twitches and hops,

a nimble dance, inches at a time. Sprigs
and stems point every which way.
The birds lack maps, but know the way

with the fewest hawks and only minor wanderlust.
I've never seen him bump his head.
She doesn't seem to scrape a wing.

They hop, peck at bark, hop again. I doubt
they imagine another day, together or alone.
This is sabbath enough, an April jubilee,
and the stores downtown have closed.

# BLESSINGS

When I respond, "And how are *you?*"
one more cashier proclaims she's *blessed.*
I look up from counting my coins.
She looks too tired to be blessed.

Later I sit among June's extravagant maples
and pines unfurling in the cozy yard out back,
seventy degrees, dry after two days of rain,
still an occasional, wandering gnat.

A small plane buzzes across my sky,
then chugs, the engine cutting out.
Someone's taking a lesson? Practicing failure?
To pantomime a crash is a blessing.

A cardinal, puffed full of himself,
tries to fill blue sky with red trill. I look up,
see branches and the charged black wire,
can't find the bird. But I got his blessing.

Inside, you pause from your busy-busy,
tending my messes and your own.
You stand in the door and your palms
stroke your ironed blouse, thoughtlessly.

More coffee? You say it as you brush
imagined crumbs from your front,
blessing yourself and me, once more,
without intent, the only way, and I look up.

# TUGBOAT

Hauling a barge of garbage out to sea,
the tug spews a black plume. I know
it stinks, but from my rented balcony
it looks elegant and soft, no fumes,
no dirt, only April silence, full of grace.

In the sand below me, a boy, about eight,
watches his mother bending in the surf
to splash her neck and face. She waves
as if to woo the boy into her cold
springtime sea, as if to say it's wonderful.

She throws open her arms
and strides toward him, dripping and smiling,
then suddenly claps her hands
to wake him into joy.
Twice she tries a cartwheel
and twice she fails, laughing.

*O, vigorous, undaunted mother,*
*take me home. I am cold,* the boy must think,
standing rigid as stone, a monument,
skinny arms folded to defend himself
against her cheer and his own shivering.

A motorboat races toward shore—
so fast it threatens to beach itself.
Maybe it's coming to save the boy.

No, it stops. Its man comes out
from under the canvas canopy
and bends over the gunwale,
searching for a thing in the sea.

Maybe he's plumbing the depths,
planning strategies to cope
with the rising moods of the warming sea.

There's no rescue. He doesn't see
the child or the mother, her hair
swirling in the breeze
as she twists and wriggles,
shaking the ocean from her skin.

The tug has traveled south a mile or so,
its long black feather of smoke
spreading into a willowy smudge,
like a flock of starlings
as they form a drifting letter S,
supple and shifting and far away.

That homey, squat, fundamental tug
could fool me into loving the sea.
Surely the captain's capable arms are hairy;
his back is broad, his face unshaven.

His daughters are six and eight.
His wife plays shortstop for the Presbyterians.
She has a game tonight, under the lights,
and he promised to be home before dark.

## MY BOY TRUTH

I was calling out for my child, Truth,
who was hiding again—under the sofa,
then behind the door.

*Where can he be?* I said, feigning drama,
so he could leap out, shouting, *Here I am!*

But he was silent. Had he melted?
Slithered under the door,
a mercury puddle, a pool of oil?

Outside I saw him narrow to a snake,
then broaden to a stream, shallow but wide,
the spongy heart of a bog, spreading.

Truth likes swamps, darkness, stink.
Once, playing alligator, he popped up
in a Palm Beach toilet. Another time

he flew skyward, dived into a black hole,
squirted out, and returned to Earth,
his obedient pet. *Good dog,* he'd coo,
patting Earth's furry head.

The other day, I failed to find him
inside the pocket of the pocket door,
which was old enough and scarred enough

to house Truth. I checked the medicine chest
where he liked to sneak my pills away
and sprinkle their dust on his yogurt.

One night, worried, I drove all the way
to the gleaming, tangled city to search,

and then the dewy suburban lawns, sparkling,
and farther still, into forever rolling hills
with farms nestled in their bosoms,
polite creeks gurgling, and eight-foot corn,
tassels hanging shiny in the dawn.

I borrowed cousin Ephraim's tractor
and chugged through alleys of corn
that whispered scary tales in the faery breeze,

till I found my boy napping
at a pasture's edge—alfalfa here, forest there,
whispering acres, nightmare trees.

Truth lay beneath a grazing cow,
beside the stalks shifting
and drying in the stir of summer air.

I scolded him, took him home for oatmeal.
I stroked his fuzzy head and implored,
*Why are you such a drifter?*

Truth smiled his pacific, un-ironic smile
and climbed the padded stairs
as if to promise he'd sleep, even without
the rustling crops to soothe him.

But he slipped out the window,
onto the apple tree, shinnied down
and trotted off without a word.

I later learned he headed for the river
at Fly, Ohio, then on west to Chillicothe's edge
(he'd always loved the name, never mind
the paper mills, the stench).

Even as I tell you this, he's on his way
to Gurneyville and Morning Sun,
walking on alfalfa leaves
and clouds. He's that light.

## ABOUT THE AUTHOR

JOHN HAZARD grew up in the southeastern Ohio town of Caldwell and now lives in Birmingham, Michigan. He has taught at the University of Memphis and, more recently, at the Cranbrook Schools and Oakland University in suburban Detroit. His poetry has been nominated for a Pushcart and has appeared widely in magazines, including *Ploughshares, Poetry, Shenandoah, Slate, The Gettysburg Review, New Ohio Review, DIAGRAM, Arts & Letters, Ascent, Atticus Review* (as Featured Poet for January 2020), *Carolina Quarterly, New Ohio Review, Harpur Palate, Tar River Poetry,* and *Valparaiso Poetry Review.* His 2015 book of poetry is *Naming a Stranger* (Aldrich Press).

CPSIA information can be obtained
at www.ICGtesting.com
Printed in the USA
JSHW020929170523
41820JS00004B/29